I am who I am because...

by

Tommy J. Chatman Sr.

authorHOUSE®

AuthorHouse™
1663 Liberty Drive, Suite 200
Bloomington, IN 47403
www.authorhouse.com
Phone: 1-800-839-8640

First published by AuthorHouse 9/29/2008

ISBN: 978-1-4343-2207-4 (sc)

Printed in the United States of America
Bloomington, Indiana

This book is printed on acid-free paper.

I AM WHO I AM BECAUSE...

Inspired by God almighty
My Lord and Savior Jesus Christ
thru by the Holy Spirit

Written by: Pastor Tommy J. Chatman Sr.
I am who I am because

Know the foundation by which you stand

Know the purpose for your creation

Live your life so God can use you

Inspirational points to better one's living now and eternal

In order to know who you are you must first
know whose you are

No matter what you are you must know whose you are

Dedication

My first and foremost dedication is to God our Heavenly Father, Jesus Christ our Lord and Savior and to our comforter the Holy Spirit. To my mother whom I can truly say is a mother. I say that because thru out my life she have shown me what a mother is and without a doubt, she is a mother. Mrs. Annie Mae Chatman. To my sisters, Carole Chatman and Catherine Chatman who at many times have helped me along the way. Supportive of me in my walk with Christ along with my mother. To my daughter Queliner L. Chatman-Benford, who has helped me with this book arrangement. To my Pastor, Rev. F.D. Clark, from whom I have learned a lot and is my spiritual overseer. Pastor William Murray who own Ole Murray's home cook restaurant in Madison, GA. Who taught me about the Bible first. While eating, he always told me about God and his word. To his wife sister Betty Murray whose always by his side. Pastor Alfred Murray of Pleasant Grove in Newborn, GA. To Pastor Joseph Nunnally of Rockhill Baptist Church and Pastor Stanley Peek of Second Baptist Church in White Plains, GA. And to everyone who have touched my life and I have touched theirs. And to the first person I told about my writing when God laid it on my heart. A very special friend: Pastor Christine Campbell Walker of Conqueror of Jesus Christ Outreach Ministry in Decatur, GA.

Thanks and may God bless you all.

Acknowledgements

First and foremost to God and my Savior Jesus Christ. Without them, not only would I not have written this book, but we would not even exist. To my mother Mrs. Annie Mae Chatman, who is ninety and still by the help of the Lord going fishing, cooking, watering the flowers, and attending church with me. Who prayed for me when I didn't have Heaven on my mind. My sisters who took care of me and still does now. Carole and Cathy Chatman. To my daughter who took part in my getting this book arranged, Queliner L. Chatman-Benford. To my Pastor, Rev. F.D Clark Sr. and other Pastors. To Wallace Grove family, Thankful Baptist family, and other church families and to all my friends.

Thank you and may God bless you.

Preface

In order to know who you are you must first know whose you are. I know people who calls on the name of Jesus, they constantly tell you Jesus said this and that. On Sunday at church they are holier than thou. They can't sit down. you can't speak because they're constantly shouting and stomping. But the next day, sometimes that same afternoon, they're degrading people, sleeping around with other peoples husbands or wives. I guess it's because they've taken off their Sunday morning outfit and put on their Sunday afternoon go getter outfit. As I say in church, one can fool me sometimes, and if they lie enough, can fool themselves, but I want you to know, you can't fool God at no time. If you're going to serve God, then serve God. If you're going to serve Satan, serve Satan. You can't be luke warm, you must be hot or cold. Either serve God or serve Satan, you make that choice. People say God gives us that choice. No, God gives us commandments and they don't change. The reason some are lost is because people have confused them. Hollowing in church on Sunday and cursing them out through out the week. I pray that whoever reads and understands this book will live their lives so that it is pleasing to God. And know without a doubt you are who you are because of our Lord and Savior Jesus Christ.

AMEN

Introduction

In writing this book I know that because of God's timing, his inspiration, his simplicity of words, his giving of certain scriptures, the title, the chapters, the length of time to write this book, my obedience to the time to write, and the ease in writing this book, I know that whoever reads this book will be able to live a more productive life. In writing this book which is the first of three (God told me one day that I will write three books and five songs) that was about a year and a half ago. I started in the summer of 2006 and it's summer of 2007 that I've finished, but not my time, but God's time.

AMEN

Table of Contents

Chapter 1
I was created

On the sixth day God created male and female. He made them in his image. The image of love which is the most beautiful thing there is. And he blessed them, and said unto them, be fruitful (reproduce in abundant) and multiply (increase) and replenish the earth. So in the process of being fruitful and multiplying, I was born (Gen. 1:26-28). God was well pleased with his creation. He allowed Adam to name the fowls of the air, and gave him dominion over everything. He told him which herb should be for his meat, and which herb should be for the beast. He put him in the garden of Eden to dress it up, make it beautiful. He told him he could eat of every tree of the garden, but not to eat of the tree of the knowledge of good and evil. Adam was obedient. Adam was doing the will of God, but Satan was able to entice Eve, and through her he enticed Adam to become disobedient (not operating in the purpose) and did the will of Satan. This brought about sin. Now we must, because of Adam sinning, we must all go thru Christ to the father. We must realize that our purpose is to worship the Lord. (Worship means to praise and glorify the Lord) So I was created to worship the lord. We must realize that the building we refer to as the church is actually our place of worship. We worship the Lord for who he is, and we praise him for what he has done. So the church is within us. Christ told Peter upon this rock I shall build my church and the gates of hell shall not prevail. Not that he want have trials and tribulations, because Job have already said: A man that is born of a woman is of a few days and filled with trouble. (Job 14:1) But they want prevail. The church which is our place of worship is holy, or any place you worship the Lord is holy. The Lord told Moses, take off your shoes you are on holy ground.(Exodus 3:5) Whether it's at a motel, school, or someone's house, it must be acknowledged as holy ground. Once you know the purpose of being created and refuse to operate in that purpose, then you are being disobedient to his word. If you continue to be disobedient to his word God will reprobate you. Reprobate means worthless. (Romans 1:28) We notice people that seems to always do things backward or wrong even thou they know to do right, they do wrong. In most cases, when confronted, they lie or blame someone else and you can't change their minds because God has reprobated their mind. Some never change, but some fall on their knees and call on the name of Jesus with a sincere heart. Lord have mercy upon me. Deliver me from my ways and instill in me your ways and instruct me to do your will. It's God will to deliver you. It's not his will that any should perish. He wants you to have life and have it more abundantly. (John 10:10) This is why we who are true Christians must tell people about God's word. God said: my people are destroyed because of lack of knowledge. (Hosea 4:6) He loves us so much that he sent his only begotten son. (John 3:16) For God so loved the world that he gave his only begotten son, that whosoever believeth in him should not perish, but have everlasting life. He sent him not to condemn us, we do that enough ourselves, but that through him, we may have everlasting life. When Christ went to the cross and shedded his blood, it was for us. He was perfect, (sinless) but he saw the condition of the world so he sacrificed himself for us. If we accept Christ as our personal Savior, (Romans 10:9) be baptized in the name of the Father, and of the Son and of the Holy Spirit, we shall have everlasting life (St. Matthew 28:19). People have different ways of baptizing, but to be baptized is to be submerged in water which signifies cleansing from sin. Some may disagree, and people are entitled to their opinion. When the Angel said unto Philip, go near, and join thyself to the chariot, Philip went and did as the spirit said (Acts 8:26-39).We as people, when the spirit tells us to do something, we debate it, refuse, take our time and gripe, because we are sometimes disobedient to the word of God. But when we need God, we want him to move immediately, and when he don't, we get upset, turn away from God and say he don't love us. Not all of us, but some of us. Yes, Christians or so called Christians. But have you thought how God feels when we disobey him? Philip went on and by doing so, he baptized the eunuch. Now remember Philip was lead by the spirit to insert himself in a certain situation which lead to the baptizing of the eunuch which was reading the scripture, but had no understanding of what he was reading. It's one thing to read the scripture, but you must get an understanding of what you read. So here we find that at that same scripture, Philip began preaching about Jesus, no doubt he was preaching about baptizing, and as they approach certain water, the eunuch wanted to know what would stop or come in the way of him being baptized. Philip said you can, but only if you believe with all your heart. And his reply was; I believe that Jesus Christ is the son of God. After stopping the chariot, they went down into the water and he baptized the eunuch. Notice here, when they came up out of the water (after being submerged) Philip was caught away by the spirit of the Lord and the eunuch didn't see him any more, and went on his way rejoicing. Once you accept Christ as your personal Savior, there's joy on the inside. Jeremiah says his words are like a burning fire shut up in my bones (Jeremiah 20:9). Notice the eunuch did not look for Philip as one might think, because the spirit of the Lord didn't let him. Now had he not accepted Christ, he would still be of a worldly spirit, and probably would have panicked, but he didn't because he was filled with the joy of the Lord. Once we accept Christ as our personal savior we still have work to do. I notice that people go to church and receive the word from on high, leave church and will not tell people on the street what thus said the Lord. As a matter of fact some want even speak to people, but will talk to someone that was there that heard the same message, from the same pastor, in the same church. That's not spreading the word, that's just having a conversation. I like talking to the people in the street, behind the liquor store, frankly they are sometimes better people than those sitting in the church. I've acknowledged that they are better people than some that I've sat in the pulpit with. They are people that's real, not fake. They believe in sharing with one another, and it's done in deed and truth (1 John 3:18). My little children let us not love in word, neither by tongue ; but in deed and truth. It's good to tell someone you love them, especially if you really do. Now telling one you love them is ok, but they should feel it and see it. You tell me you love me, but you see me hungry, and want offer me anything to eat, see me walking, and want give me a ride, that's just talk. Not knowing I'm hungry, you offer me food. Not going in my direction, yet you go out of your way to drive me where I'm going, that's love. And that's what the world needs more of so that the light in us will shine and the people of the world will see. We ask the question, what's wrong with the people of the world? There's nothing wrong with them. The problem is with Christians or so called Christians. God made the birds, birds fly. He made the fish, fish swim. He created man to serve him. Man, not all of us, but some of us, worship everything but God. Some Pastors come to town and there's no vacancy in any hotel. Not pointing at the pastors, and people have their preference, but I know some pastors that have been preaching in town for years and truly preaching the word of God, and more people will go to the club than to church. What I'm saying is people, not all, worship the creation more than the creator. And we say what's wrong with the people of the world? Worldly people do what worldly people do. We who are called by his name is not serving the Lord the way we should. They see in some of us what they do. So why stop their ways when some of our ways are like theirs? In some cases, their ways of treating people is better than some of the people in church. They speak, try to help you in any way they can, and do it with a smile on their face. They are the same every time you see them. Some church goers, bench riders, show casers, holier than thou, fashion wearers speak to those that are on their level, help those that are equal or richer than themselves or people that are nicely dressed like themselves. They must not realize that, they're not just doing it to them they're also doing it to the Lord (St. Matthew 25:42-46). This is not to say all Christians are like that, shouldn't be any, but Satan has his people in church too. Yes. From the Usher that smiles and speaks to some, and act as though they're talking to someone or looking for someone, not to speak to others. Congregation members who don't want you to sit beside them. Deacons who think they run the church and you're not on their level. Mothers on the mother board who, because they have been on the board awhile and wears pretty cloths, look at you like you're less than them. Pastors in the pulpit that talk to some and not others, go to some houses and not others, have been preaching longer and thinks you're less than him. Yes it's true. Hopefully someone will remind

5

them that they're no better than anyone else in God's eyes. Maybe in man's eyes, but not in God's eyes. We're all like filthy rags and have come short of his glory. Sometimes people are so familiar with you as a worldly person that they want look beyond who you was to see whose you are. Not because they can't see whose you are, because when Christ changes you, everyone who knew you, know you've been changed but because there is no Christ in them, they don't understand the Christ in you. If you don't know blue when you see blue, you might say it's green. Certainly you want say it's blue. In some cases people just want you to keep your self-esteem low so they will look bigger. We sometimes think we are more than people in the street because we dress better and have more money. Let me tell you something about life, you can be up today and down tomorrow (you can be rich today and broke the next). The only thing that stays the same is God's word. It never changes. The wages of sin is still death and the gift of God is still eternal life. I look at movie stars and singers that look for love from someone with the same statues as theirs. Mainly because if the person (mostly men) feel equal to the women as for as status, if he loses her he feels he can get another woman because of who he is. And vice versa. If your looking for love, you must look beyond material things, the outward appearance, and the type of job one has. I know we have preference, but don't let that limit you. I feel we miss being in love and finding our soul mates because we don't except a person for who they are. But for what they are or what they have. True love is from the inside and it shows on the outside. True love is not identifying yourself with a person of great status, but identifying yourself with Jesus. Some pastors and I were talking in the pastor's study and they began to talk about the problem with the flag. I understood what they were saying, but I had to let them know that, that flag identifies you. I don't identify myself with a flag, but with the cross. They march about the flag, but will not go into the street and say anything about the cross or Jesus. That flag want save anyone, but accepting Jesus Christ as your Lord and savior will. We must tell the people about Jesus. We as Christians, and not all of us, I use the word we , but I know I'm not included, will talk about everything except Christ. We will help everyone except the one that truly needs help. We visit everyone except the sick and we say we love God. If we truly love God, we would do or try to the best of our ability to do his will his way. We must realize that it's not about us , but about God. It's not so much as where we are, but where we will spend eternal life. Not how long we lived, but how we lived as long as we lived. Did we show love in our everyday walk? Did we help people along the way? Did we say an encouraging word to someone? Did we tell someone about the lord? Did we let them know that the only way to the Lord is through Jesus Christ (St. John 14:6)? Did we let them know they're never to low for God because he sits high and looks low? That he stands at the door knocking (Rev. 3:20). Did we tell someone that if they open the door and invite him into their life, he will come in and there will be a change? You may not feel it immediately, but after awhile you will. When he comes in he clean up the inside because he will not dwell in an unclean place. He moves the negative thinking from your mind(the thinking that you will never be nothing) and replace it with positive thinking. I am somebody. I am a child of the most high God, and I can be anything I want to be thru Christ Jesus. Acknowledge him in all thy ways and he will direct your path (Proverbs 3:6). That's how we show the world whose we are and show God how much we love him. Let them know it was not me who changed me because I was in my comfort zone and had no intention of moving. But God changed me and I know that without a doubt. If he changed me he can change you if you let him. He is no respecter of a person (Acts 10:34). He loves the man in the ditch as much as he loves me. Sometimes we as Christians want the world to think we are better than they are, but they are God's creation also. All of us was created to worship him. It makes no difference how long you have accepted Christ as your Lord and Savior, but that you accept him. You'll have the same right to the tree of life as one who accepted him 100 years ago.

Thanks be unto God our Father and our Lord and Savior
Jesus Christ And the Holy Spirit our Comforter.

AMEN!!

Chapter 2
I was born

God created man on the sixth day and from that creation we were born. We had a divine time to be born, but we were born from the initial creation. The birth of each generation started the birth of the next generation. We, who was born of this generation, was ordained for this generation. We of this generation probably could not have made it in the time of four or five generations ago. In fact we probably wouldn't make it four or five generations from now. Look at the people of yesterday, they worked in fields sun up to sun down, rarely got sick, and when they did they used herbs to heal themselves, and the well helped the sick. Now people have all kinds of sickness and if they take medicine for it there's a side effect. You heal one problem and cause another one. No one is going to help you unless it's family, and sometimes they want unless there's money involved. Unless we who are called by his name get on one accord and do God's will, God's way, there may not be a fourth or fifth generation from now. Our birth has a purpose, we might not know now and some never will know what it is, but there is a purpose for our life. My being who I am is no coincidence. You being who you are is no coincidence either. God told Jeremiah: before I formed thee in the belly, I knew thee: and before thou camest out of the womb I sanctified thee, and I ordained thee a prophet unto the nations (Jeremiah 1:5). Before we were thought of, God knew us and he had a purpose for us. We wonder why things don't go right on our job, it may not be what God wants for us. Since the pay is good we put up with problem after problem. Have you asked God, is this what you want for me or am I operating out of my purpose? God wants one to be an Usher in the church, but we want to be a Deacon. God wants to elevate you, yet you're content where you are. So God has to stir up something in your comfort or accepting zone in order to move you. Until we begin operating in our purpose there's going to be a problem. Now even if we're operating in our purpose it don't mean that we want have a problem. Job said: a man that is born of a woman is of few days, and full of trouble (Job 14:1). You will have trials and tribulations as long as you live. We don't know how long we have to live, but sometime between birth and death, which is life as we know in the flesh, we're going to have some problems. Some we cause on ourselves and some by others. Weeping may endure for a night, but joy cometh in the morning (Psalms 30:5). Night is our dark hour, losing a loved one, someone very ill, someone in distress, someone prison bound or having a relationship torn apart brings sad times, but after a while when the <u>son</u> shine, (yes the son s-o-n, the son of God, not the sun), he will give you joy. You may have thought you couldn't make it, but now you're on your way. You may have thought you couldn't live without your husband or wife, but now your in a new relationship, and you didn't know what joy was, because you only knew about happiness. Happiness is of the world, and is temporary. What made you happy yesterday, you have to do again to make you happy. But joy! Joy comes from the Lord, the giver of every good and perfect gift (James 1:17). As the song writer says: this joy that I have the world didn't give it and the world can't take it away. But the happiness that the world gives, the world can take it away. Being blessed with the love of God, his grace and mercy, good health and strength, family happiness, a new home, a new car, money in the bank, and a great job is from the Lord and all the glory goes to him. God wants us to have these things, but we must not make them our God. He will have no other God before him (Exodus 30:14). I don't know about anyone else, but Balaam can't do me like Jesus. Balaam can't bless me like Jesus, Buddha can't heal me like Jesus and Muhammad can't speak to me like Jesus. Jesus is the only name in heaven and earth, whereby man can get any help. As long as we feel like this job pays well and we have a new house and a new car, making more money than both our parents made in one month we accept the situations that comes with the job. Let me say something, I'd rather make $200.00 a week and have peace, than to make $2000.00 a week and can't rest, and don't have social time with my family, and especially with my God. One might say I make more than my family did, but look at the pictures, your family may not have had the opportunity that you have. They might have had to sacrifice something so you can have a better opportunity, or more so they knew what was more important. Serving God first and with the strength of the Lord meeting the needs of their family, keeping their family together and trying as much as possible to keep them happy with the joy of the Lord. It's good to have nice things, but the greatest thing to have is Jesus as your Lord and Savior. You might make more money than your parents, but if you don't have peace, love, or joy in your life, you don't have nothing. What good is it to have nice things, but on the inside you're hurting and your family is torn apart because you're always tense and under pressure. Your husband or wife is gone, your children are afraid to ask you a question because every time they do you snap. Money's not that important. Making less money and having time to serve God and having quality time with your family, having peace, love, and having joy within is more precious than having a few more dollars. For what is a man profited , if he shall gain the whole world, and lose his own soul? What shall a man give in exchange for his soul (St. Matthew 16:26)? The answer is nothing. You can't carry anything with you when you die. A man brought nothing into this world and certainly he will carry nothing out. Salvation is not exchangeable, non purchasable and the greatest thief in the world can't steal it. The only way to receive salvation (assurance of eternal life) is by accepting Christ as your Lord and Savior (Romans 10:9). Only thru Christ can we have eternal life. No man or woman can go to the Father unless it's thru Christ. I am the way, the truth and the life, no man cometh unto the father, but by me (St. John 14:6). I'm glad God made it that way. No matter how much money you have, how good looking you are, who your people are, where you live, how often you go to church, your position in church or how long you've been in church, you still have to go thru Christ by accepting him as your personal savior. He's no respector of persons (Acts 10-34). God loves the man in the ditch like he loves the Pastor in the church. God loves us all. It's ok to make preparations to live a good life on earth, that's what God wants for us. But without a doubt, the most important preparation one can make is preparing to live with Jesus. Not just you but your family, children, neighbors, even your enemies as well as your friends. Talk to them about preparing to live with Jesus. Not tomorrow, but now. Tomorrow is promise, maybe not on this side, but it's promised, and where you live eternal life depends on your preparation today. Your preparation will determine whether you live in Heaven with Jesus, or in hell with Satan. Choose this day whom you will serve (Josh 24-15). Not tomorrow, not next week, but now. So when the triumphant sound in the sky sound, when the dead in Christ rise, and those who are alive shall be caught up together with them in the clouds, to meet the lord in the air: and so shall we ever be with the lord (1 Timothy 4:16-17). But we must make preparation now, not later. The past is gone, the future is not yet, all we have is right now. After we have made preparation and gotten ourselves ready, we must tell someone else how to get prepared. I'm not talking about people who was in church with us, because they had the same opportunity to hear the word as we did. I'm talking about lost souls that are in the hedges, on the corner, behind the liquor store and even the ones in our own homes. I'm not talking about that quick word or a word of high education, but constantly telling them in words they can understand. They may not respond immediately, but keep telling them. You see we at first hearing the word didn't accept Christ as our personal Savior, so we can't expect them to. God was patient with us, so we must be patient with them. It's not when you accept Christ, but that you accept Christ. It's not what you was, but what you are. It's not who you are, but whose you are. I once was lost, but now I'm found. I was lost in a world of sin, and on my way to Hell but someone was praying for me and God answered their prayers. Now thanks be unto God, I'm found and on my way to Heaven and I want turn around. I'm waiting patiently for my God and Savior. I got my house in order and my mind made up. I, without a doubt will make Heaven my home. We don't want to talk about dying, but as sure as we were born we are going to die. That's an appointment we all will keep. You can break appointments with doctors and reschedule, but not this appointment. And as it is appointed unto men once to die, but after that is the judgment (Hebrews 9-27). You see when we were born we had no knowledge of this, but as we grew people began to tell us about the word of God. I don't know about anyone else, but I was told about

God's word time and time again. Not that I didn't hear the word, I just didn't want to accept it. Even if you are in the world and someone tells you something about the word, time something happen those words will convict you. Then you instantly remember God's word. So shall my word be that goeth forth out of my mouth: it shall not return to me void, but it shall accomplish that which I please, and it shall prosper in the thing where to I sent it (Isaiah 55:11). If you hear God's word and do wrong the word will convict you. We always say something told us not to do something or not to go here or there, but lets not call it something, but call it what it is, the Holy Spirit. I remember setting in Ole Murray's Restaurant eating breakfast and there was Rev. Murray, Rev. Bishop, Deacon Tolbert and sometimes others. As they talked about the Lord, I was listening and the word began to stick in my mind, and I began to get confused. Some things I thought was right was totally wrong. Because I ate in this place almost every morning, I began to understand because I started asking questions. Because they were willing to explain things to me, and I mean truly explain, I began to have a thirst for God's word. Because of the thirst for his word it became routine to meet in the restaurant in the morning, midday and some evenings. We never sat a time to meet, but God did. Even though I had to go to a job, I stayed there until we met and I got a word. We began to have conversations there and I began to see with a spiritual eye how good God is. I thank God for these men, whom he sent there for this purpose, because God, thru them was preparing me for his work. Rev. Murray and his wife Mrs. Murray has some of the best home cooked food I've tasted. Sometimes I would drive from Norcross to Madison, GA. Just to get their food. Almost a one hour ride, but his food don't compare to the bread of life. Earthly food will make you swell, and swelling sometimes goes down, but when you eat the bread of life you grow and the more you eat the more you want. The thing about this bread is that it want make you sick, overweight, want give you high blood pressure, and want send you to the doctor, but if digested properly it will give you love, peace, joy, sound mind, and most of all salvation (the right to the tree of life). For every action there's an equal and opposite reaction. There's day and there's night, there's good and there's bad. What I'm saying is there was always one that came in that represented Satan, who always tries to put doubt. He was a highly educated man, a retired teacher of science. When you're anchored in the word of God, when you've accepted Christ as your personal Savior, no one can uproot you. Not anyone. My sheep hear my voice, and I know them, and they follow me: and I give unto them eternal life; and they shall never perish, neither shall any man pluck them out of my father's hand. I and my father are one (St. John 10:27-30). No man having put his hand to the plough, and looking back, is fit for the kingdom of God (St. Luke 9:62). Once you know God's word, not just hear it, but know his word, then you must continue in it and abide by it. Once you know God's word and abide not in it, then you will be chastised with many stripes and he who don't know will be chastise with few stripes. Either way if you do wrong, whether you know or don't know, you will be chastise. The level of knowledge of God's word determine the level of chastisement. In other words if you know better, do better. Once I accepted Christ as my Lord and Savior I began to understand that the things I thought I was doing, giving myself the glory, I started giving the glory to whom it's due, my Lord and Savior Jesus Christ. I understood that if he didn't allow me I couldn't do anything. I'm here because of his mercy. Justice say we should all be dead, but his mercy allow chance after chance and I thank Jesus Christ for going to the cross. In this world today we're a modern day Sodom and Gomorrah. We ask what is wrong with the people in the world? The answer is nothing. The problem lies with us, we profess that Jesus is our Savior, but we want talk to the people in the world, but we will talk about them. We'll point a finger, but we want lend a hand. Some claim to be afraid of the people in world, but remember someone talk to you when you were in the world. We don't say anything to children when they're wrong, but someone said something to us. Yet we say greater is he that is in me than anything in the world (1 John 4:4). I remember going out to Wallace Grove Baptist Church because the water in the baptizing pool weren't circulating, at least that was what one of the deacon thought. I went out to check on it and as I looked into the pool, the spirit of the lord got hold of me and let me knew that, this was the church he wanted me to join. 10 o' clock the next morning I was going in the water to be baptized. I accepted Christ that Saturday after checking on the pool. Looking back, it was God's way of bringing me to that church, which was God fearing, Christ served, Bible based and filled with love. He knew I would be happy there. Every church you see with a steeple on it don't mean that Christ is the center, or it's Bible based. I thank God for sending me to a church where love is in deed and in truth(1 John 3:18). Where people show you that they love you, and don't just talk it. After joining Wallace Grove, I started learning God's word by studying, going to Sunday school, which is the planting bed, Bible study, where you can ask questions and get a understanding (Proverb 4:7). Don't just read, get a understanding of what you've read. When people tell you something you don't understand, ask them to explain it until you do. I realize that the Pastors at the restaurant and my Pastor Rev. F.D Clark, Rev. Crew, and others were preparing me for my purpose. They were instilling in me the word of God and making preparation for God to elevate my calling for me to be a Pastor. I was ok just being a member, but because of my obedience, God was able to prepare my heart and mind. The church chose me to be set aside for a Deacon, and after that I was ok being a Deacon, but God said you're still obedient, and now I'm going to elevate you to Pastor. Now I know why I was born. Now I must sow a good seed in some good soil, so I can wreep a good produce.

Thanks be unto God and our Lord and Savior
Jesus Christ and the Holy Spirit.
AMEN

Chapter 3
I was nurtured

When you're born you have no idea of who you are, why you're here, or when you will die. From the moment you're born you begin a process called living. There's certain things that your mother or who ever is attending to you begin to do in order for you to survive. This is called nurturing (providing the necessities that comes along with living). Providing milk, changing diapers, holding you in their arms, and talking to you. Without these things rarely one can survive. Understand, children don't ask to be brought into this world, it's the result of a man and woman's sexual actions. Part of replenishing the earth. Once here it's both the man and woman responsibility to nurture them. In so many cases when the baby is born the man leaves the woman, and sometimes before the baby is born. There's still a must that the baby be nurtured. But sometimes the baby is discarded or aborted. We know this is wrong, but sometimes these are worldly people and they think it's ok. Christians should never let that be a thought, certainly not an option. One of the most beautiful things there is, is the birth of a child. Along with that comes responsibility in order for that child to grow. So if a man and woman engages in sexual activity knowing that there's a possibility of a child, if God allows the child to be born, then the right thing to do for both parents is to nurture that child and raise it the way they should. So that once that child is old he want depart from it. Not that once he is older he want stray, but if you raise them in the way that God instructs us, the word will convict them when they stray, and do wrong. There are responsibilities for parents to train them up in the way of the Lord (Proverbs 22:6). People say the sin of a child is on the parents until they are twelve years old. That's as far from the truth as east is from west. Christ had to come down thru forty-two generations to bare our sins. If we could bare our sins he wouldn't have had to come. His coming was to bare the sins of the world. If we can't bare our own sins, how can we bare the sins of our children? People say that when a child dies at two to three years old they go to hell. I don't know where they get that from, and I don't profess to know the whole Bible, but the God I serve, the only true and living God, would not be a God that loves his children, and let them die and go to hell. These people have truly been misled. And if they truly know God then they would know that it's not his will that any should perish (2 Peter 3:9). So if a child, having no knowledge of it's own existence or a person of old age having no knowledge to understand how to make a decision about their salvation, God is not going to keep them out of Heaven. God loves us to much to do any wrong. Same as parents, we discipline our children because we love them. When I was young growing up in the neighborhood every one of age were your parent. When you did wrong they whipped you, and when you went home mom or dad whipped you, sometimes both. It didn't kill us, actually we're more humble people. Now if you discipline a child the wrong way you'll be charged with child abuse. If they had child abuse when I was growing up, some of the parents on Hancock St. might be just now getting out of prison. And they ask what's wrong with the children of today.

Look at the system today, if you hit one you're going to jail. The word says he who spare the rod hateth his son; but he that loveth him chasteneth him betimes (Proverbs 13:24). If a person don't love a child they don't care what they do. Chastising is a part of nurturing a child: withhold not correction from the child: for if thou beatest him with the rod, he shall not die. Thou shalt beat him with the rod, and shalt deliver his soul from hell (Proverbs 23:13-14). We must not let the government instruct us as to how to raise our children. Certainly we must not abuse them, and I totally agree with that. Some people go too far and cross the line between discipline and abuse. People are afraid to whip their children because they are afraid of what the government will do. I understand that we have the law of the land, but it's the law of the Lord that we must obey. The law of the land is sometimes different from the law of the lord. If I'm obeying God's law, man may put me in jail, so be it. Man has no Heaven , nor hell to put me in. Even when we do right, we are sometime mistreated by the government. Sometimes they know they're wrong and still cause misery. That's why I just obey God's law, and if man is right, his law will line up with God's law. You see, God will never cause you misery for doing right. Certainly things happen to us when we're doing right, but somewhere down the line we've done wrong. God don't always punish us the moment we sin. Sometimes God allow things to happen to us for a testimony on down the road. If you deliberately do wrong, that's not God. God is love, and love will not allow you to hurt anyone. The Lord told the children of Benjamin: stand ye in the ways and see, ask for the old paths, where is the good way, and walk therein and ye shall find rest for your souls (Jeremiah 6:16). If we start walking in the path of yesterday when everyone were your parents, when you could leave your doors unlocked, when you could eat at anyone's house, when children played with one another and not hated one another, and when parents were parents and let children be children the world would be so beautiful and a great place to live. The Lord said: if my people. which are called by my name, shall humble themselves and pray, and seek my face, and turn from their wicked ways; then will I hear from Heaven, and will forgive their sin, and will heal the land (2 Chronicles 7:14). We who are true Christian are the key, but we must first get ourselves right. Pastors not liking other pastors because one can preach better or dress better, or one has a larger church. We must be supportive of one another. If a pastor isn't doing right, then talk to him, but first make sure you're right. If he don't listen carry someone else with you. And if he still don't listen, then pray about him and let God handle him. It's not about any of us, it's about God. So instead of talking about the pastor, talk to him. In other words we must be about God's business. Nurturing a child is part of it. We must get it right with the Lord so he will heal this land so that our children and our children's children will have a better place to live. But we, not the people of the world, must obey God's word and I know we will see a change because I know God don't lie. As they get old by the grace of God and can understand, we must start instilling in them the word of God. Start bringing them to church, not sending them. Let them participate either in the choir, Usher board, or welcome address. If we don't give them something, satan has a lot to give them. He will be glad to nurture them. That's why I say let them participate, give them something to do so they want just sit there idolizing. There's a time in their life while growing up they'll take on their own identity. Sometimes they stay on the right path and sometimes they will stray. You can be the best parent in the world and raise your child the right way and they will still stray. But at some point they will come back to the way they were raised. Sometimes God will reprobate them when he constantly tell them that they're doing wrong and they continue doing wrong. (Romans 1:28) says: and even as they did not like to retain God in their knowledge, God gave them over to a reprobated mind, to do those things which are not convenient. For not the hearers of the word are just before God, but the doers of the law are justified (Romans 2:13). Just hearing the word does not justify you, but hearing the word and doing the will of God will justify you. That does not just apply to children, but parents also. We as parents must not provoke our children to do wrath, but bring them up in the nurture and admoration of the Lord (Ephesians 6:4). Children you must obey your parents and the Lord: for this is right, honor thy father and thy mother; which is the first commandment with promise, that it may be well with thee, and thou mayest live long on earth (Ephesians 6:1-3). We must tell them the word of God and make sure they understand as best as possible. We must see that they walk in a Christian like manner. Talk to your family daily about God's word. Have prayer with them, let them pray, and let them read the Bible and explain what they read in the Bible. Ask them questions, and let them know you also need answers because you being an adult don't mean you know it all. Let them know that we also had a pass, we weren't always Christian. We've done wrong in our life time, but somewhere along the line we got on the right path and turned our lives over to Jesus. Let them know that if they want eternal life they must accept him as their Savior. Mother can't do it for you, and your father can't do it for you. It's an individual thing you must do for yourself. The same path the lady at the well took when she told her people, come, and let me show you the one who told me all about me, everything I ever did (St. John 4:29). Because she knew he was Christ, she lead others to him. That's what we must do. Bring them to church and when we lift up the name of Jesus in our devotion, our

23

singing, and our preaching, Jesus will draw them. Jesus said: if I be lifted up I will draw all men unto me (St. John 12:32). If he's lifted up his word promises to draw all men unto him. Once you're on the right path, don't look back at the pass because if you look long enough you'll begin to sink in it. If God delivered you from drugs and you look back at the pass, at the good times you had in the world doing drugs, stealing and robbing, after a while you'll begin to turn back and before you know it you're doing the same thing. The pass is just that, but it's your future that means something. Preparing to go with Jesus when he return. We in the church must nurture you until you're able to understand. Once you come into the spiritual rem of God, you're not familiar with your surroundings and it's easy to step back into the world, because you're familiar with the world. That's why churches must be about God's business. When people come out of the world and into the church and see pastors sleeping with this member tonight and another tomorrow night, deacons at odd with the pastor because they're sleeping with the same member and they're both married, mothers fighting the ushers over the pastor, men sleeping with men, and women sleeping with women will turn people away from the church. Some are coming to church looking for salvation and all they see is what's going on in the world. We must stand for Christ or we will surely fall. If I stand for Christ and people don't like me, it's ok. I have my house in order and my mind made up and I have no doubt where I'm going to spend my eternal life. I was nurtured by my mother, my sisters, the people at Wallace Grove, Rev. Murray, Rev. Bishop, and Deacon Tolbert until I was able to grasp God's word and understand what it meant. Now that I know God's word and understand what it means, I'm living my life according to his word as best as I can. I fall sometimes, but I get up. I don't complain about my fall because if I'm up all the time I want know how good it is when he deliver me. I want have a reason to call on the name of Jesus if I'm always up. I call on Jesus whether I'm up or down, in the sunshine and in the storm. I let him know I thank him for all that he do. I thank him for holding my hand so I don't let go of his hand. Jacob had a pass, but he wrestled with a man and he wouldn't let go until he blessed him. The thing I like about God blessing you is that there's a sign, a showing, and not only that, but he changed Jacob's name to Israel (Genesis 32:22-29). That's why we must be the light Christ wants us to be so people in the world can see the light in us. Our life must be an example of Christ. We must let our light shine before men, so that they will see our good works and glorify our father which is in Heaven (St. Matthew 5:16). We all like light because it makes it easier to see. Walking in darkness is not impossible, but it can inconvience you and cause you to stumble and fall or run into things. Being a Christian mean you're on the greatest path of your life. Not only is your path full of light, but it shines bright and it will shine on someone else who is in the dark. Like the song say: there may be someone down in the valley waiting to come home. Your light may be the only light someone sees. Some say, and I've heard it from the pulpit, that it's hard to be a Christian. I don't know and I'm not trying to find out what type of Christian they are. It's easy to be a Christian. How hard is it to love someone, how hard is it to help someone in need and do right? Now professing to be a Christian and still living a worldly life probably is hard. The key to that is being who you are. If you're a Christian, be a Christian; if you're a crook, be a crook. Whatever you choose, be that. If you choose to serve the Lord, then serve him and give him your best. After all Jesus is the only way we can go to the father, the only way. If you choose to serve Satan, then serve him and be prepared to live with him in the lake of fire and brimstone. Choose you this day whom you will serve (Joshua

24:15). Our service to God begin after we leave our place of worship. The problem I find in some people is that they're selfish, self centered, they share with those whom they can get something in return, they'll do for the pastor if they like him, but those they can't get something back from they want help them and don't want the church to help them. If no one in the church family is in need, or they gave someone something last week they don't want to give them anything this week, and want to send it to the bank. Missionary money should never be kept. If there's not a need in church, then give it to someone in the community. Use it for what it's taken up for. We then, that are strong, ought to bear the infirmities of the weak, and not to please ourselves (Romans 15:1). We all get weak sometimes and I don't care how powerful you think you are, at some point in time you'll get weak. This is the time we're in need for help. I feel that if you help someone in need truly from the heart you're planting a seed. When you plant a seed which is single, it will multiply itself at the time you wreep it. So plant a good seed in some good soil and you will wreep a good produce. In other words , if you help someone who truly needs it, not only will you be blessed, but God will also bless your children. So many times pastors preach what thous said the world, and not what thous said the word. What Sally and Sue does is not our business, nor what Mickey and Mike does is not our business. If one is doing wrong then we must tell them. Now, how you tell them is how they will respond. The Lord said: by my loving kindness have I drawn you. So you can't approach them any type of way. We must let them know that God's word says: for this cause God gave them up unto vile affections: for even their women did change the natural use into that which is against nature, and likewise also the men; leaving the natural use of the woman, burned in their lust one toward another. Men with men working that which is unseemly, and receiving in themselves that recompence of their error which was meet (Romans 1:26-27). Eve was for Adam help meet, not Steve. We say for God I live, and for God I die. If we truly mean that then we will tell people that this is wrong. We would show them this in the word and make sure they understand it. And if they don't want to receive it, then dust off your feet for a testimony against them. Let us not be like Peter, Lord I love you and three times he denied him. If we're going to preach God's word, preach it. And if someone is doing wrong then the word will just have to convict them. If they have a problem with it, then let them take that up with God, but you be obedient and the blood want be on your hands. We must let them know this is wrong, but if they repent, God will forgive them. We all have done wrong, but the key is repentance. Pastor going against pastor. Pastors saying women is not suppose to be pastors, women can't sit in their pulpit. We need to support Pastors who are doing God's will and not envy them. I don't, but some Pastors say God didn't call women to preach, but some men he didn't call, but you let them in the pulpit. Some say women can't preach because she can't be the head of the church, neither can men, Christ is the head and Pastors are in charge. That's where we get it mixed up. We think the Pastor is head, some Deacons think they're the head, and some think their money is the head or their family. No, we truly need to get that right. Jesus Christ is the head and we need to acknowledge that. The word say: many Pastors have destroyed my vineyard, they have trodden my portion under their foot, they have made my pleasant portion a desolate wilderness (a deserted wilderness). They have made it desolate and being desolate it wreep unto me; the whole land is made desolate, because no man layeth it to heart. Those who have been nurtured right should keep it right. I'm not just talking about gay men and women I'm talking about all of us. We may not be gay, but if we lie and lust after the flesh, we sin.

27

There's no little sin or big sin. The charge is still the same; death, and it don't change. What I'm saying is quit envying one another and quit downing a Pastor because you have more or you preach better then him. We must embrace one another and if we see one making a mistake, tell him, not the world. Time out for foolishness, we need faith, time out for entertainment, we need encouragement. Too many lives are being lost because we haven't gotten ourselves together, doing God's will, God's way. It don't matter how much money you have or how well you preach. This is the reason worldly people don't come to church. They see more foolishness in the church than out there in the world. Let's nurture like we've been nurtured so that we can win over some people to be saved. Judgement is going to start in the house of the Lord. We who are Pastors must get it right, then our congregation will get right, and then after we leave those walls we will be glad to spread God's word. We must be willing to nurture people when they come in so they will go out and tell someone else. That's the way to get it right and now is the time. Be truthful to one another and God will be truthful to us.

Thanks be unto God our Father Jesus Christ our Lord
and Savior and the Holy Spirit our Comforter.

AMEN

Chapter 4
I was given mercy

If you're living, still existing in the body in which you were born, maybe not as young, maybe not as many teeth as you once had, and you may have lost a limb or an eye or ear, but still in the same body, it's because of God's mercy. Let us understand the meaning of mercy. Mercy is: giving or receiving care when it's not deserved. But God, who is rich in mercy, for his great love wherewith he loves us even when we were dead in sins, hath quicken us together with Christ (Ephesians 2:4-5). But understand, when we want mercy, we must come boldly before the throne of grace, that we may obtain mercy and find grace to help in time of need (Hebrews 4:16). Justice says we all should be dead, but mercy because of God's love and Jesus making intercessions for us have allowed our golden moments to ride on a little while longer. And certainly not because we deserve it. We as Christians, not all of us, or maybe I should call it the way it is, those bench riders, those fence stratlers, those one day Christians, not those truly trying to do the will of God. We want God to have mercy on us, but we don't want to have mercy on anyone else. If God has mercy on us, why can't we have mercy on someone else? We can think of all the reasons in the world not to help someone and can't think of one reason why we should. So you don't have to think of one reason, let me tell you one. Jesus. One said can anything good come out of Nazareth? The best thing in the world came out of Nazareth, our Lord and Savior Jesus Christ. While we were yet in our sins, Jesus died for us. Not that he had to. He was at his home on high, perfect. He didn't want us lost, because he had a love for us, more than we do ourselves, he gave us mercy. So if you can't think of one good reason, then you're not a true Christian. You may profess to be or act like a Christian or go to church every Sunday, but if you don't have love in your heart, forgiveness, sacrifice, or self denial, you maybe religious, but not a Christian. A true Christian is Christ like, trying to do the will of God, God's way. Grace which the Lord say is sufficient and mercy is given to us daily. We're not here because of ourselves. That's the problem with most people, they think what was done was by self. I was at one time the same way. I thought what was done was by me, but when I accepted the Lord as my Savior and began to get some knowledge about him, then I understood that it wasn't me, but the Lord working through me. Now, I acknowledge that it was the lord. When I was in a world of sin, it was the Lord. When I would have been in a certain place, and satan had a trap for me or I thought I just didn't feel like going and stayed at home and things happened there, I now know it was the Lord. When someone plan to hurt you, and for some reason you had to leave, it was the Lord, or you should have gotten off on a certain exit, but you missed that exit so you went another direction and you later found out that there was a sniper targeting all the cars coming down that street at that time, it was the Lord. That's why I thank the Lord daily for his grace and mercy. That's why I ask God to hold my hand so I want let go of his hand. So that I want return to adultery, hatred, lying, deceitfulness and things such as to cause sin. Am I perfect, no, none of us is perfect, but I'm truly trying to do God will and do it his way. That's all God wants from us to give him our best. He's given us his best, so why wouldn't he want the same in return? The word says: no man, having put his hand to the plough, and looking back, is fit for the kingdom of God (St. Luke 9:62). Simply put, once you grab hold to God word and turn back to the sinful things that you once did, then you're not fit for what God has for you. Once you leave the world of sin, return only to tell someone who is still lost, the word of God. And think not before time what you need to say. In the same hour God will put in your mouth what to say. So we need not practice what we're to say unto them. If we study God word, in Bible study, Sunday school, even at home the word says: study to show thyself approved unto God, a workman that needeth not to be ashamed, rightly dividing the word of truth (2 Timothy 2:15). When you tell someone in the world that the wages of sin is death (and that is the wage that will never change), but the gift of God is eternal life (that's a promise that will never change). Let them know that God, whether we know it, or whether we admit it, God gives us grace and mercy everyday and not because we deserve it, but because he loves us so much and that he wants us to be with him in paradise (Heaven). That's why it's so important that we constantly tell the people of the world about God and our Savior Jesus Christ. We must let them know that we have all been in the world and we have all done wrong, and if grace provide we will do wrong again. The difference is that when we were in the world we sometime chose to do wrong. Now that we have accepted Christ we may do wrong, but it's not intentional, we don't choose to, but sin can be so small that sometimes we sin because we're unaware of it. That's the difference. But I let people know that I know God changed me and that he's no respector of a person (Acts 10:34). He'll change you. He stands at the door and knock: if any man hear my voice, and open the door, I will come in to him and sip with him and he with me (Revelations 3:20). He's knocking daily, but he want break in, you must ask him to come in. He wants to be our Lord and Savior. And we must let them know this. That's why I constantly tell them about Christ, because he didn't stop knocking at my door and finally I accepted him. So I can't stop telling people about Christ and his goodness. I pray for loss people in the world daily, not just here in America, but everywhere, not just my family, but everyone. People are falling by the wayside daily and it's mostly because they don't know about the Lord. The Lord says: my people are destroyed because lack of knowledge (Hosea 4:6). If we keep telling them about the Lord, they may receive him, but even if they don't, at least they will have heard. Everyone is not going to receive his word. Some don't even want to hear the word, but we, who are true christians must tell them about what thus said the Lord. I look at society and I see that Jehovah Witnesses, say what you want about them, they are persistant in telling you about the Lord. One may not agree with their message, but you must agree with their method. They try to make sure that they do what they believe and if you don't want to listen they know that they have done their part. We as other denominations, will talk to people who were in church with us about God's word, but will not go into the world and tell the people of the world. That's what's partly wrong with society today. They think because people are on the corner or behind the liquor store that they're too good to talk to them or too good to be in their mist. Let me tell you something, I personally have found that the people behind the liquor store are better than some in the church. Those in the church will help those who can help themselves, or they associate with people that are on their level or have as much as they do. The people you see behind the store share with one another, they love one another, and not because of the liquor bottle, but because they truly love one another and they show it. So if we talk to them about God, and that's something that I do, and you'll know when the time is right, and you'll know when it's time to stop. But in talking to them, you'll find that they know about Christ but don't want to come to church because of how some people are in church. And I sometimes agree. Sometimes they tell me exactly who they are talking about, and I know who they are. They see the same thing in the church that they see in the street so they want come. But God still have mercy upon them also. We think because we're not sick or have more than enough or we're warm when it's cold, cool when it's hot, and smiling most of the time and we look around and see people not doing as good as we are, we, some of us, think it's because of what we're doing or who we know in the flesh. It's not because of what we're doing, most of us are doing wrong most of the time. It's not who you know, sometimes the people you know do wrong more than you. But those who are true christian know it's because of his mercy. Justice says that we all should be dead. But his mercy says give them another chance. If it wasn't for his grace and mercy we would not be here. As the older people say, if it was not for the Lord on my side where would I be? That's so true. We have Christ as our advocate (one who pleads the cause of another). The word says: my little children, these things I write unto you, that ye sin not. And if any man sin, we have an advocate with the father, Jesus Christ the righteous (St. John 2:1). The thing is some take the blessing of the Lord in the right way and some use it in the wrong way, some complain that it's not enough, and some blessings are not even from God even thou they profess that it is. The word says: every good gift and every perfect gift is from above, and cometh down from the father of lights, with whom is no variableness, neither shadow of turning (James 1:17). So even when we feel that we don't deserve

God's blessing, he still blesses us. He woke us up this morning, maybe not in the best of health, but he woke us, only because of his grace which the word says: my grace is sufficient for thee: for my strength is made perfect in weakness (2 Corinthians 12:9). I don't know how anyone else feel, but I deserve what God gives me. People say I don't deserve what God gives me, well thanks be unto God who know just what we deserve, because if that was true you would not have woken up this morning. I make mistakes, I fall down, but I don't stay down. That's why I ask God to hold my hand so I want let go of his hand. It's his grace that have brought us thus far and it's his grace that will lead us on. I truly understand my singing when I sing amazing grace. I understand because I know it was his grace and mercy that kept me. I was in a world of sin, and on my way to a dying hell with Heaven nowhere on my mind. But one day! Oh, one bright Saturday evening, I was touched in a way that even with the best explainable word in the dictionary, I couldn't explain how good it felt, but thanks be unto God our father and our Savior Jesus Christ, while I was on my way he paused me long enough to make an intelligent decision and accept Christ as my personal Savior. I was called out to the church to check on the baptizing pool, but when I looked into the water the spirit of the Lord caught hold of me and eleven years later haven't let go. I know it was the Lord. I didn't change over night and there's still some cleaning and pressing to do unto me. I'm climbing Jacob's ladder and every round gets higher and higher. Before when people done me wrong, I'd plot to get them, Now I'll pray, but sometimes I still want to get back at them. I'm just being real. I find that most people I have problems with are in the church and the worst problems have been with pastors. I have personally come in contact with some that when you try to help the church they deliberately try to do you wrong and hide their hand. They suppose to be leaders, but are worse than people on the street. I know I have to pray for them, but sometimes this flesh makes me think differently, but I pray because I know that vengence is the Lord. When I get like that I ask the lord to have mercy on me. Not because I did anything, but because I wanted to do something. You see I've done wrong and the Lord had mercy on me. So when someone do me wrong I have to ask God to have mercy on them. When Christ went to the cross he said: father have mercy on them for they know not what they do. Even though they did him wrong, he, not them, asked God to forgive them (St. Luke 23:24). Stephen, when he kneeled down and cried with a loud voice, Lord, lay not this sin to their charge. And when he said this he fell asleep (Acts 7:60). So even though you're trying to do the right thing for Christ, there's always someone trying to stop or distract you. And most of the time it's people who profess Christ as their Savior, wolves in sheep clothing. But when you can ask God to have mercy on someone who you know is deliberately trying to do you wrong, then you will know God has created in you a new heart and renewed the right spirit. That separate the Christians from church goers, people with that one day religion which they take off and put in the closet for the next six days. Even with them God still have mercy on them. Oh, I thank God for his mercy, not just for me, but even for those who don't ask for themselves, because I too was one of those people. Grace said give him another day, and mercy said I'll give him joy.

Thanks be unto God our Father,
Jesus Christ our Savior and the
Holy Spirit our Comforter.

AMEN

Chapter 5
I asked Jesus to be my Savior

Jesus came to earth for the purpose of redeeming mankind. The word redeem means to save, to recover through or by payment, to deliver. The song writer says: my redeemer lives. Christ came thru forty two generations, hung, bled, and died for us. And he did it because he loved us. And God allowed him because he loved us. For God so loved the world, that he gave his only begotten son, that whosoever believeth in him should not perish, but have everlasting life (St. John 3:16). Everlasting life don't begin after you die as some will have you think, but it begin once you accept Christ as your personal Savior. If thou shalt confess with thy mouth the Lord Jesus, and shall believe in thine heart that God hath raised him from the dead, thou shall be saved (Romans 10:9). If you ask Jesus to be your Savior, and believe on his name he'll come in and he'll be your Savior. When he comes in he's going to do some cleaning. You know we use the phrase spring cleaning. Jesus will do some temple cleaning and also set in order some things. He begin upstairs where you store hatred, dislike, non-forgiveness, meanness, and idolatry senseless thoughts, in other words, he'll get your mind right. Box all the foolishness in boxes and put them outside. Then to the bedroom and remove fornication, adultery, and sexual immorality, he'll box that up and put it out. Then to the kitchen where he boxes your eating disorders. We've become a generation that will eat anything we want and God has certain things for us to eat. Fruits with seeds, and certain types of meat whether from the sea or land. So he boxes up our eating disorders and puts them out. He goes into the living room where cursing, fighting, disrespect, negativity, and evil worshiping is lying around. He box them up and put them outside. Now you're like a house when no one lives there or no one occupies the home, it's vacant. And that's how you feel because you're used to having company. Now Christ replaces all that with his word. Now can your house be calm, holy, joyful, prosperous,but most of all, God fearing. Christ had to put all of that out because he want dwell in an unclean place. Not only is he coming in, but also the father. Now there's going to be some people that will look into the boxes that God put out, and they're going to tell one another, I knew he had this and that in him. But we must understand that it don't matter what we had in us, but who we have in us. We all have done wrong, we all have had issues in our life whether we admit to it or not. So let them look. I find that people, and some of them profess Christ, will look way over good to see bad. So let them look so they can see we've been changed. I came to Jesus as I were and he changed me. I know without a doubt Jesus changed me. I was comfortable as I was. But at some point I wanted to know the lord, but I kept making excuses because I hadn't changed myself. But then I decided to go to the Lord as I was. I tried to change, but I couldn't so I went to him as I was. I didn't surround myself with true Christians, I didn't talk to my mother or sisters about it so I didn't know. But I came to the lord because he made a way. I thought it was me, but it was really the Lord ordering my steps. He knew my heart. Now I tell people, don't wait until you change, let God change you. Just tell the Lord I need you to change me, because I can't do it myself and I ask you to be my Savior. Right then, if you are sincere from your heart, God will. You may not see a change at that moment, but there is a change and it will effect you for the rest of your natural and eternal life. I came to Jesus as I was, I was weary, wounded, and sad, oh, but I found in him a resting place and he has made me glad. Amazing grace how sweet the sound, that saved a wretch like me! I once was lost but now I'm found: was blind, but now I see. In order for God and Christ to make abode with us, we must first love him and keep his words: if any man love me, he will keep my words: and my father will love him and we will come unto him and make our abode with him (St. John 14:23). God wants us all to be a participant, he says: whosoever will, let him come. Come to him weary, wounded, or sad. God's not concerned about your fleshy condition, but rather your spiritual condition. God knows that even though the outside has worn, and been abused the inside which is preserved by the outside is still the same, untouched. That's why we need God to create in us a clean heart and renew the right spirit. God deals with the inside. The potter takes the same clay and rework it until he has it the way he wants it. In other words God uses the same body, but he works the inside again and again. The heart I had I couldn't love everybody, the spirit I had was evil, but after Jesus became my Savior and cleaned my inside up I was able to love everyone. I have the right heart, I'm passionate and compassionate, I have the spirit of the Lord. I look for good in people, I thought positive, I didn't talk about people, I talked to them, I didn't point the finger, but I handed the hand. The way you treated people years ago have to change, and not only will you know it, but people around you will know eventually. When there's a change in your life, and people see it, it's sometimes hard for people to receive that you have changed because they're looking for familiar actions from you. And it's understandable because that's what a person has shown. But when God changes you, you are truly changed. when Saul was converted to Paul, straightway he preached Christ in the synagogues, that he is the son of God. But because of his past, when he was bounding the people, they didn't believe him. All that heard him were amazed, and said: is not this he that destroyed them which called on his name (the name Jesus) in Jerusalem, and came hither for that intent, that he might bring them bound unto the chief priests (Acts 9:20-21)? The people asked the question because they wanted to know if he was fooling them, trying to lure them in. They knew the devil had tricks they haven't seen and some they will never see. But certainly they saw a difference in his professing. You know some people profess Christ, but there's no Christ in them. Because they can quote the Bible don't mean they know Christ, they may know of him. Even satan himself knew the Bible and could quote the word. And he brought him to Jerusalem, and set him on a pinnacle of the temple, and said unto him, if thou be the son of God, cast thyself down from hence: for it is written, he shall have angels charge over thee, to keep thee: and at their hands they shall bare thee up, lest at anytime thou should dash thy foot against a stone. And Jesus answering said unto him, it is said, thou shall not tempt the Lord thy God (St. Luke 4:9-12). So you see, satan knows the word. When we have accepted Christ as our personal Savior, when satan comes up against us, and as sure as we live, he will, we can tell him: get thee behind me satan in the name of Jesus. We must understand that greater is he that is in me than any that is in the world. Ye are of God, little children, and have overcome them: because greater is he that is in you, than he that is in the world (1 John 4:4). Christ is not in everyone, only those who have truly accepted him as their personal Savior. If thou shalt confess with thy mouth the Lord Jesus, and shalt believe in thine heart that God hath raised him from the dead, thou shall be saved. For with the heart man believeth unto righteousness; and with thy mouth confession is made unto salvation (Romans 10:9-10). For God so loved the world that he gave his only begotten son, that whosoever believeth in him should not perish, but have everlasting life (John 3:16). If we are to be saved, we must believe on the name of Jesus. When I think of the name of Jesus it puts a smile on my face and joy in my heart. Jesus the name above all names. Jesus my Lilly in the valley, my bright and shining star. My way out of no way. Jesus my all and all. When ever in need, Jesus. When I'm in my valley, Jesus. When I'm on my mountain, Jesus. King of kings, Lord of Lords. My fortress, my strong tower, my portion. He's everything I need. When all you got is Jesus, you got all you need. Any sickness, he's able to heal it. Any problem, he's able to solve it. There's something about calling on the name Jesus. I called on my mother, she being a mother, she did all she could, I called on my brother, he did what he wanted to do, but when I went down on my knees and looked toward Heaven and called on the name Jesus, he did just what he said. Mothers will do all that they can for a child, that's a mother. Now because a woman births you, don't qualify her as mother and because a man helped it does not make him a father. And the king said: bring me a sword. And they brought a sword before the king. And the king said, divide the living child in two, and give half to the one, and to the other. Then spake the woman (the mother) whose the living child was unto the king, for her bowels yearned upon her son, and she said o' my lord, give her the living child, and in no wise slay it: she is the mother thereof (1 kings 4:24-27). The true mother was willing to give up the child than for it to be slain. The other woman, not being a true mother didn't care. Jesus loves us more than that. He loved us so much he hung, bled, and died on Calvary's cross for us. He died that we might have a right to the tree of life. To choose life, we must choose Christ. I am the way, the truth, and the life, no man cometh unto the father, but by me (St. John 14:6). I thank God for his son Jesus being my Savior, and giving me the opportunity to get myself prepared for Heaven. We must understand that Heaven is a prepared place for prepared people. Jesus said: in my father's house are many mansions: if it were not so, I would have told you. I go to prepare a place for you. And if I go and prepare a place for you, I will come again, and receive you unto myself; that where I am, there ye may be also. So if one wants to live with the Lord, he has to do some preparing here while breath is still in his body. I wish everyone would accept him as their Savior, I really do, but I understand that that's not going to happen. But I truly believe that if we in the pulpit quit speaking negative things about one another, quit disliking each other, stop bragging about who has the most members or who has the most beautiful church, and start lifting each other up in prayer, start speaking kind words about each other and deacons begin to understand that they are not in charge of the church, the pastor is. When the mothers start being mothers and teach the young ladies of the church how to be young ladies for the Lord so they will know how to be ladies for their husbands, and stop trying to take each others husbands, so that the congregation will see the light in us and start to walk in the light. I truly believe we could go into the world and win over some souls that are lost. But as long as the deacon is overrunning the pastor, the pastor intimate with members or the congregation and mothers fighting in the church, why would people in the world want to come in the church? The same thing happening in the world is happening in the church. People are confused. How will they accept Christ? How shall they call on him whom they don't believe? How shall they believe in him whom they have not heard? How shall they hear without a preacher? How shall they preach, except he be sent? As it is written, how beautiful are the feet of them that preach the gospel of peace, and bring glad tidings of good things! We must be about God's business, doing his will and doing it his way. There's some people who wants to be in church, but we have people in church thinking because they have the smell of liquor on their breath or clothing is not suitable to them, they want to put them out. The lord said whosoever will let them come. We must not allow that kind of foolishness to prevail at church. They might have been to the club last night and that's where they accepted Christ or they may be coming to church trying to get right, but they don't have cloths that look as good as ours. But that's no reason to put them out. If we are to be Christ like, then we must not be concerned with the outward apperance, but the inward. God says: by my lovely kindness have I drawn ye. And that's the way we must be. Nobody put us out, not to say some of us don't need to be, but we must let them hear the word of God. So then faith cometh by hearing, and hearing by the word of the God (Romans 10:17). That's why we should speak to all people about God's word. Everywhere we go we must tell someone what thus said the Lord. I believe that if we do that and let the light inside of us glow, more people will accept Christ as their personal Savior. Let us get on one accord and do God's will and do it his way.

AMEN

Thanks be unto God our Father, Jesus Christ our
Savior, and the Holy Spirit our Comforter. Thanks
be unto everyone who is doing God's will.
We, together can make a world of difference.

Chapter 6
I acknowledge whose I am

In order to know who you are you must first know whose you are. In order for me to know I'm a Chatman, I must first know truly that my father is a Chatman. I don't care what name you're given, you are truly what your father's name is. If I say I'm a Chatman and my father is not a Chatman, then the name I use is not truly my name. it's a name that for one reason or another was given to me, or at some point in my life, I chose to change it. If one says he is a child of God, then God has to be his father. Our father which art in Heaven hollow be thy name. hollow be thy name means that it is set aside for holly use. We are speaking of our heavenly father (God). I often times hear people, mostly pastors use the word daddy. To say our daddy is not giving the honor to God. My word says our father, not our daddy. So if the word doesn't say daddy and we use it, then I think we do an injustice to God. A daddy plants the seed, but a father accepts responsibility for the welfare for his child. A daddy can be a father, but a father will not be referred to as a daddy. Being a father is not just biological. A father is a father to other children in the community, in the house hold, and a woman may have children by someone else before they met. But if he's a true father, when he accepts the mother, he accepts the children too. It's a package deal. In many cases people know who their biological daddy is, but they acknowledge who their father is. I knew who my daddy was, but I acknowledge who my father is. My father is God almighty. I acknowledge whose I am. I am a true child of God. People may say different, but when you're a true child of God, you acknowledge whose your father, then it matters not what people think or say. It's what you know and God loves. Even though the light of the Lord shines bright in your life, there's always going to be someone who will speak wrongly about you. That's because they're jealous, envious, or just don't know God themselves. There's some people that go to church and call on the name of Jesus and don't know God. Even though that sounds strange, it's true. They know of God, but to truly know God, is to have an intimate relationship with him and our lord and Savior Jesus Christ. If you don't know who your father is, then you don't know who you are. But when you know who your father is, then you can acknowledge him and let everyone know that he's your father. Children love their fathers, their mother too, but I'm speaking of the fathers. The father plays an important role in their children life. When you are a true father, your wife and your children look up to you for strength. You're the bond that keeps things together. Even in frightening situations, they feel more at ease when the father is present. A father is the link that keeps a family together when it's about to fall apart. That's why I call God my father. When I can't seem to make it, he assures me that he brought me yesterday, surely he'll bring me today. All the encouragement one needs is to understand that he brought you yesterday, certainly he'll bring you today. His word says I will never leave you, nor will I forsake you (Hebrews 13:5). No matter how dim the light seems, it's still light. When a child is obedient, the father wants to do for them, he wants his child to call on him for strength, for guidance, for encouragement, for love. When a child feel the love of their father, they're not afraid to talk to him because they find comfort in him, even just being in his present. And that the way it is with God. He's our father. He wants us to call on him. I call on him just to let him know that I acknowledge that he's my father. I call on him daily. Thru the good times and the bad. I thank him while joy is in my heart and when storms come people don't know it because I still call on him. He supply all of our needs, but for those who tries everyday to live by his commandment, he'll give them the desires of their heart. Delight thyself also in the Lord: and he shall give thee the desires of thine heart (Psalms 37:4). Our father want us to call on him, he wants to provide for us, but he wants us to do right. Doing wrong causes sin, and the wages of sin is death. In the early days back in the sixties, that's when I remember, men took roles as fathers and woman took roles as mothers and they didn't have to be your biological parents. Now if you look at the community today, some are not being fathers or mothers to their own children, so certainly they can't be to anyone else. The Lord told the children of Benjamin to stand ye in the ways, and see, and ask for that old path, where is the good way and walk therein, and ye shall rest for your souls. But they said we will not walk therein (Jeremiah 6:16). In that old path, not that they were perfect, but parents cared about children and they looked out for them. Any person of age could discipline you if you were wrong and your parents didn't question them. I know sometimes they were wrong, but I wouldn't say nothing. But I said when I have children I was not just going to listen to the adult, but to the child too. I'm glad I have that mindset because adults will lie on children and intentionally mislead them. My daughter was in her last year of school and a problem occurred, and she need that class to graduate. She was suspended and she called me. When you talk to your children, most of the time you know when they are lying.

I didn't feel she was lying and I called the school for a conference. Not at all speaking from a racial point of view, but an adult point of view, even though the teacher was white and my daughter black. There was an assistant principal which I believe was from another country. I had a chance to talk to him first. He assured me that he thought a lot of my daughter and he didn't think she would behave like that, and that she was very well mannered. In this meeting was my daughter, the principal, the assistant principal, two counselors (a male and a female), the teacher and myself. I understand that there's good and bad in all of us. Being the father that I am, I wanted to hear both sides. I learned while I was young that fathers should protect their children, provide for them, look out for their well being. So I listened to what the principal said, and she felt the suspension was justified, the woman counselor also. The male counselor didn't say much, but I found it strange that the principal (not the assistant principal) and the counselor decided to make a judgement on what they thought had happened. They asked my daughter to apologize, and before I could say anything, my daughter said I'm not apologizing and I haven't done anything wrong. Then she said daddy you can punish me, but I want apologize for something I didn't do. You know your child, and I knew she was telling the truth. I told them to let the teacher speak, she tried to remember the lie she had told, but it didn't come out right, so then she broke down and told the truth which was just as my daughter stated. I flew off the handle then, because the pricipal and counselor made their decision based on what the teacher said and when they found out she lied, instead of them doing the right thing, they got an attitude, and so did I. I said that to say that people need to hear both sides. If your child is wrong they're wrong, and punish them, and let them know they can't do wrong, but if they're right you stand up for your children. That's what a father and mother does. God loves us so much that he gave his only begotten son, but when we do wrong he chastise us, but when we're right he will fight our battles and that's the way parents must be. I thank my father (God) for strengthing me and making me who I am. If I was like parents of the old, I probably would not have believed my daughter and she was right. God being the father that he is, when people do us wrong he let us know that vengeance is mine. Just let God handle the problem. The old testament speaks of an eye for an eye, but God says stand still and know that I'm God. What ever our situation is, take it to the Lord and he will handle it. And that's what a father does when someone hurts his child.people don't need to mess with God's children. Touch not mine anointed, and do my prophets no harm (1 Chronicles 16:22). The difference with God taking care of his children is: he'll revenge for his children and nothing can be done about it. That's why it's important when you're defending your children, that you're right. Some people defend their children and know without a doubt they're wrong. Sometimes, as senseless as it maybe, sometimes people are hurt, even killed. If we as parents approach people in a Godlike manner, the situation, most of the time want get out of hand. There's two sides to any problem or situation. The word tells us to be quick to listen and slow to speak. People have probably went to their graves defending their children knowing in their heart they were wrong. But because they thought their children couldn't do any wrong or their children wasn't at fault, and they defended them, they're dead and their children are doing the same things. God is not like that, and I'm glad he isn't. He'll defend us when we're right and chastise us when we're wrong. That's the way we must be when situations come about with our children. Don't make them think that every time they do something you'll defend them whether they're right or wrong. You're giving them the wrong message. In other words you're telling them they're right when they're right and they're right when they're wrong. We must raise our children in the right way, the way God intended and we must do it while they're young. While you have them in line, because once they get old, they take on their own identity. Even though one raises their children up in the right way does not mean they want stray. I've seen that in most cases the children have been taught right and lived right, but as soon as they become of age, they stray. Some say that it's the pressure of being young. I can agree in some cases that may be true. I feel even though they were raised in the right way, doesn't mean they will stay on the right road. Let me show you what I mean. at a young age, between six and thirteen, I went to Sunday School and sometimes church. But after a while I stopped. At this time, the school teachers was well to do, faired well, and upscale. The reason why I stopped was because the teachers would talk about some of the kids which was less fortunate than they were and at a young age, I knew that was wrong and teachers being adults should not talk about children in that manner. I tell people now, if you see someone less fortunate than you, instead of pointing your finger at them, give them your whole hand and help them. Instead of talking about them, talk to them. Self examine yourself. If you can't do this from the goodness of your heart, then you need to kneel down on your knees and ask God with a sincere heart, to create in you a clean heart and renew the right spirit within you (Psalms 51:10). If one says that they're a true child of God and want help someone in need, then you are just an outside show to the world and you're not acknowledging whose you are by the life you live. There's a song we sang that say, may the work I've done speak for me, may the life I've lived speak for me. The work you've done do follow you. We're either hot or cold, we can't be lukewarm. Either we serve God or we serve satan. The work that you do will speak for you. That's why some kids grow up and stray. They see what some grown-ups do and they record it. And at sometime they will play it back. They may act right around you, but when they're not around you they act out or hit playback and that which they recorded comes out. And if they hit playback enough they will begin to act it out. They stray, but if you planted the right seed while the soil (the child) was right, they may stray, but they want depart. The seed is the word of God. Once they receive it, if they do wrong it will convict them. Not just children, but parents also. When you're a true child of God, and you know whose you are and you acknowledge whose you are, then you need to let your light shine. I know without a doubt that I am a child of God and people around me know I'm a child of God because my actions speaks for itself. I don't have to carry a Bible, even though I do because that's my instructions, and I don't have to wear a cross, even though that's what I identify myself with, just how I treat my bretheren will speak for me. Some people say they are of the black race, white race, and the Spanish race. I'm of the human race. You see when we say we're of the black, or white race we separate ourselves, but when we acknowledge that we're of the human race, then we're together. The same can be said about religion. I often ask pastors: if we're serving the same God, and the same Jesus, then why are our messages so different? I understand that we may have different methods, but our message should be the same.

Thanks be unto God our Father, Jesus Christ our
Savior and the Holy Spirit our Comforter.

AMEN

51

Chapter 7

I've gotten my house in order

In order for your house to be in order, it must be operating in the divine order of the Lord (righteousness). If I've gotten my house in order, it must have been out of order (not operating in a God like manner). I'm talking about God's temple, this earthly house. Getting yourself operating like God intended, worshiping and serving God everyday and not just on Sunday, not just calling on him when trouble arise, but thanking him even when nothing is wrong. When it seems like everything is well because someday there's going to be a storm. When the storm rise and the wind blows, will you still have joy? Will you give him thanks? Will you still praise him? In all things we must still count it a joy. No matter what your circumstances are, there's someone worse off than you. But when you can still smile, still praise the Lord, and still thank God thru Jesus Christ, then your house is in order. In the house you reside in whether it's yours by yourself or with a family, there's an order which is given by instructions of the Lord. Man is the head, no exception, his home must be operated in a Godlike manner. Understand that God don't dwell in unclean places. So if you want God in your house it must be clean. The husband is the head of the family, he covers his family. In other words he is responsible for the welfare of his family. I remember even when I was still in the world, I loved thunder and lighting, and rain, we were sitting in the bed talking and the rain came about, with it was heavy lighting, and roaring thunder and my wife would jump around my neck with a tight grip because she was afraid. It was funny to me, but I realize that she felt safe in my presence. She could be up the hall in the kitchen cooking, and I knew if it thundered one time she would be coming down the hall. I said that to say, the family feels safe in the husbands presence. That's why we must serve God at all times because our family looks to us for guidance and strength. The wife have responsibilities also. She must leave her family and cleave to her husband. When they twain, they become one. Now because God made man as the head, doesn't mean he's always right. God gave the woman a brain also. So you can think for yourself. But God must hold someone responsible and he chose the man, the husband, which is the stronger of the two vessels. In the garden he called Adam, he gave instructions to Adam, not Eve because Adam was the head and the wife is his help meet. There's some things man just can't do, therefore the woman helps him. But when this is not operating the way God instructed, the house is out of order. This is why homes have so much trials and tribulations in and around it. It's out of order. The wife working two jobs, coming home after work, cooking and cleaning, but the husband is at home all day or in the streets with his friends and contributing nothing to the home, the woman having to make all the decisions, it's always going to be a problem there because it's out of order and satan has stepped in. When Job had his wife close to him satan couldn't persuade her, but when he got the opportunity he quickly tried, but Job held on to his integrity. Though he slay me yet will I trust him (Job 13:15). The wife must be submissive to her husband as unto Christ. This means that if the husband is lead by Christ, and she's willing to be led by Christ, which means following rightousness, then she shouldn't have any objection to being led by her husband because he's led by Christ. So if she follows and accept his saying, then not only is she saying yes to her husband, but because he's following Christ, she's also saying yes to Christ. That's being obedient and you're operating on one accord and God is in the mist. Then will the relationship flourish and people will rejoice in seeing it because it's the work of the Lord. When God is in the mist of something, it's beautiful, loving, peaceful, prosperous, and joyous. But don't think everyone will be happy. Satan and his team is watching and planning. But remember it's not what people think, but what God loves, and if God's for you, who can be against you. The husband likewise has a responsibility (love your wife as I have loved the church). Love, first of all will cover a multitude of sin. The wife is not always right in her thinking, neither is the husband. They both will make mistakes. The husband must love his wife inspite of her down falls,inspite of her outward appearance (no matter how beautiful she is today, maybe not tomorrow, but her beauty is going to change). In other words you must love her from the inside, not because of how she look or what she has, eventually that's going to change but the inside (the church) will stay the same. Christ told Peter on this rock, I will build my church and the gates of hell will not prevail. Not the rock on the ground, but Peter's heart, his inside. The place referred to as the church is our place of worship. The church is within us. So the husband must love his wife unconditionally. The husband attending one church and the wife another, or the husband attending church and the wife staying home doing something that's not Christ like. That's not the will of God. (St. Matthew 18:20) says for where two or three are gathered together in my name (Jesus) there I am in the midst of them. Therefore when the husband and wife is on one accord, Jesus being the focus or center point, everything will flow smoothly. When children are involved, there's a responsibility concerning children. (Proverbs 22:6) reads, train up a child in the way he should go and when he is old, he will not depart from it. This mean teaching him the word of God, and showing him the right way. We must understand that this doesn't mean they want stray. We can do our best and sometimes they still stray. But if you have done what is according to God's word, then the rightousness of God is in him and the word will convict him, and usually they will surrender to God. Then there's a responsibility for the children, honor they mother and thy father: that thy days may be long upon the land which the Lord giveth thee. Also fathers and mothers provoke not your children to wrath (anger/get mad), but bring them up in the nurture and admonition of the Lord. Nurture means (care/nourish) and admonition means (advice or instruction) of the Lord. In other words rear them in a God like manner. (Ephesians 6:1-4). I truly believed that, if a family pray together, they will stay together. Not so much living under the same roof, but staying connected to God, staying in touch with one to another. Strength is in unity. Fathers should lead the family in prayer, but also teach his family how to pray and what to pray for. Not always asking the Lord for something, but most of the time, ask God, what will he have you to do for him this day? Most people don't ask God what they can do for him, because we know that he will tell us to feed the hungry, visit the sick, take care of the widower, and so on. We as parents must speak positive words to our children because the word you speak or the seed you plant will take root and grow. Speak inspiring words to one another. I can do all things thru Christ which strengthens me (Philippians 4:13). When you know that the Lord is your strength and you acknowledge him in what ever you do, no matter how dim the light looks, no matter how far away it seems, the promises of God will be delivered. The psalmist said: it is better to trust in God than to put confidence in man (Psalms 118:8). Know that in your going thru, and we all go thru some things in our life which seems like we want make it thru, but after prayer and trusting in God, we're on the other side and didn't realize we had came out. Yea though I walk through the valley of the shadow of death, I will fear no evil: for thou art with me; thy rod and thy staff comfort me (Psalms 23:4). Sometimes we go thru things that will break or have broken some people down. We have sickness that cause some people to die, we have accidents that have killed or badly injured some, but because of our Lord and Savior we have come through, still whole, not because of who we are or how much money we have, but because of the mercy of the Lord. God is no respector of a person (Acts 10:34). He loves us all the same, not like man, which sometimes loves his family, friends, or someone of his same status, but those that are less fortunate than them or sometimes have not been in church as long as them, they tell them stand by themselves, come not near to me; for I am holier than thou. The Lord says these are the smoke in my nose, a fire that burneth all the day (Isaiah 65:5). In Christ there's no little I's and big U's. If one accepts Christ today, he has the same right to the tree of life as someone who accepted Christ 100 years ago. If thou shalt confess with thy mouth the Lord Jesus, and believe in thine heart that God hath raised him from the dead, thou shalt be saved (Romans 10:9). For with the heart man beliveth unto rightousness; and with the mouth confession is made unto salvation (Romans 10-10). The Lord tells us, it's not so much when we accept him, but that we accept him as our Lord and Savior. The word says serve him in your youth, while the evil days comes not, when one begin to take on himself to follow after worldly thing, following satan, doing things that are wrong and evil. Nor the years draw nigh. When you've become of age and have served satan all your workable days and is able to do nothing for yourself nor anyone else and God, then you want someone to wheel or tote you into the house of the Lord, but when you was able to serve as deacon or on the usher board or even as pastor, you was serving satan, now you want to call upon the name Jesus. The great thing is, God is not like man, that's why I thank him for being the God that he is and Jesus who he is, less we all would be lost (Ecclesiastes 12:1-8). Choose God this day, and get your house in order and serve him in a way that is pleasing to him.

Thanks be unto God our Father,
Our Lord and Savior Jesus Christ,
And our comforter the Holy Spirit.

AMEN

Chapter 8
I live so God can use me

When we think about it, our purpose here is to worship God. He made man to worship him and him only. But if you look around, man is worshiping everything except the Lord. I must say that not all of us is being disobedient, but for those that are, the Lord says: I will have no other God before me. We must understand, some people worship their wives, some worship their money, some their possession, and some the pastor. They worship the creation more than the creator. Eventho he wants use to love our spouses, our car, our pastors, our friends, and yes, our enemies, he still wants us to understand that we must not put any one or anything before him. We must try to the best of our ability, to live a life that is pleasing to the Lord. None of us are perfect. For we all have sinned and came short of the glory of God (Romans 3:23). We sin sometimes unknowingly and sometimes intentionally. Things come up against our flesh that makes us sin. But we don't have to. Satan destroyed many that belonged to Job even his body. God instructed satan not to touch his soul. Job was dealt with harshly by satan. Job said naked came I out of my mother's womb and naked I shall return thither: the Lord gave, and the Lord hath taken away; blessed be the name of the Lord. In all this Job sinned not, nor charged God foolishly (Job 1:21-22). If Job sinned not after all he went thru, why then do we think we have to sin? There's a saying; we are in the flesh and the flesh is of sin. So we are going to sin. Job was a man in the flesh like we are. Yet he sinned not. But when we sin, we must first acknowledge that we have sinned. Then we must repent. Not just saying it, but ask God for forgiveness and truly mean it from your heart. You can tell yourself a lie so long that you believe it, but no matter how long you lie, God knows it's a lie. We must live our lives so God can use us. Live a life that is pleasing to the Lord. Then saith he unto the desciples, the harvest truly is plenteous, but the laborers are few; pray ye therefore the Lord of the harvest, that he will send forth laborers into his harvest (St. Matthew 9:37-38). When Jesus saw that they wanted to know God, and there was no one telling them about the word of God the way they needed to hear it, if they heard it at all, and when he (Jesus) saw the multitudes, he was moved with compassion on them, because they fainted, and were scattered abroad, as sheep having no sheperd (St. Matthew 9:36). God has sent his pastors to teach and preach his word. Because someone stands in the pulpit and is the pastor doesn't mean he was sent by God. I don't care how he preach, or how good he knows God's word, he can't preach unless he's sent by God. He may entertain, and give a good show. Notice sometimes when someone tells you about a preacher they heard, they'll tell you he preached today, and he had people falling out in the church. They were running up and down the isles, boy, he preached. Ask them what he preached on, what the sermon was and notice, at first they were all excited, their excitement has gone and they're looking foolish. I've been to a church where the same people run up and down the isles, same people fall out, and the same people speaks in tongue. They put on the same act every Sunday. The preacher running around in church from one side of the pulpit to the other.up and down the isles healing the same people. He touch them and they fall out. If God heals you thru me, then I must give the glory to God. Why do people need healing every Sunday? Why is it the same people? God does not half do anything. So we must understand that it's all an act, entertainment. I tell the pastors, the spiritual overseers, that we must support one another, but only if we are doing God's will, God's way. If you are acting a fool, I'm not supporting that. So many are falling by the way side because they don't have any direction. They come to church looking for an answer, and what they see is a dressed up version of what's happening in the world. They realize it immediately and they get discouraged. So they return to their familiar place. The harvest is truly plenteous. People need Jesus, and they come to church and the people in church are acting a fool. That's why we who are true worshipers pray that God sends forth some pastors that will lead, guide, teach, and care for his children. Some pastors were ordained by God before they were born. Before I formed thee in the belly; I knew thee; and before thee came out of the womb I sanctified thee, and I ordained thee a prophet unto the nations (Jeremiah 1:5). God have already chosen his pastors and when he's called, you'll know it. But some have chosen to serve man instead of God. They're worried about how many members, how big the church, or the type of people that come. I can truly say; I'm not concerned about how many people come to church, but how many accept Christ as their personal Savior and serve him. I'm not concerned about one's money, their position, who their people were, their status in the community or how good looking they are. All of that is temporary and it want get you to Heaven. The only way one can get to Heaven is by believing in the name of Jesus. How then shall they call on him in whom they have not believed? And how shall they believe in him of whom they have not heard? And how shall they hear without a preacher? And how shall they preach, except they be sent? As it is written, how beautiful are the feet of them that preach the gospel of peace, and bring glad tidings of good things (Romans 10:14-15)! Understand that the word of God says; how can you preach except you be sent. Faith cometh by hearing, and hearing by the word of God (Romans 10:17). In order for people to trust in God, they must first hear the word of God. We need pastors to stand boldly on the word of God and preach the word of God in the way that is pleasing to God, so that God can do a work in people lives thru faith. No matter what you are going thru you need faith. Without faith it is impossible for you to please him: for he that cometh to God must believe that he is; and that he is a rewarder of them that diligently seek him (Hebrews 11:6). But you know , even with the foolishness of preachers some are still being saved. For after that in the wisdom of God the world by wisdom knew not God, it pleased God by the foolishness of preaching to save them that believed (1 Corinthians 1:21). So let us be the people that God can use, let us be a vessel for God so that by us and thru us his word will be edified. Saul lived a life in a way that God knew he could use him. Saul was a man that whatever he did he did it to the best of his ability. His mission was to do harm to God's people. God knew that if he change him he would have the same approach. When he changed him to Paul, he was just as bold about standing on and preaching God's word, that's why it's important that God change us and not we ourselves. We must understand that God says; I will bless them that bless you, and I will curse them that curse you (Genesis 27:29). Therefore anyone in need and you're able to help them, do so. While the ark was at Obed-edom house everyone who was there was blessed, everyone who was associated with him were blessed. Blessed by association. On the other hand, anyone who is cursed if you associate with them participating in like manner with them, you will be cursed. That's why I love being in the presence of people who truly love and worship God. I'm no more or less than anyone, but negative thinking people, I stay away from. Some people always seem to be down, but they profess Jesus is their Savior. I know we all fall sometimes, no matter who you are, but even going thru my trials and tribulations I still have joy. I have problems, but most of my problems is the knowledge of other people problems. Once I know of others problems, it's on my mind until it's resolved. If you live so God can use you, God will do something in your life that the world can't understand. I remember after my wife went to be with the Lord, that hurt me more than any physical pain had or could, but I remain stedfast in God's word. I understood that it's once appointed to man to die, then comes judgement. Even though it hurt, I knew that we all must leave. I knew that to be absent from the body is to be present with the Lord. I know where she is. I also knew that I had to continue with my faith in the Lord. Because I had a personal relationship with the Lord, I was able to stay on course. I still presented myself as a servant for God. Thru my trials and tribulations, I still had joy. I was still a living vessel for the Lord. After which I was set aside for the office of deacon. And after that the Lord called me to the ministry and I am still serving the Lord faithfully and I pray I stay that way until God calls me home. I know the life I live will speak for me. HALLELUJAH!

Our life will speak for us in the way that we live.
We must understand that it's not how long we've
lived, but how we lived as long as we lived.

Thanks be unto God our Father, Jesus Christ
our Savior, and the Holy Spirit.

AMEN

Chapter 9

I'm no more or no less than anyone

You know there's people that think because they have more than you or they look better than you they are better than you. To anyone who feels or have felt that way, know that God didn't make them any different than you. He created all of us alike. And God said, let us make man in our image, after our likeness. So God created man in his own image, in the image he created him; male and female he created them (Genesis 1:26-27). And God saw everything he had made, and behold it was good. And the evening and the morning was the sixth day (Genesis 1:31). God created us the same. Your worldly wealth may make one think that they're better than you, but never let anyone make you think they're more than you. They may possess more than you, but that don't make them better than you. You are no more or no less than anyone. It's not what you have or how you look, but how your heart is that makes the difference. What you have or how you look is temporary. That's why God deals with your heart. If your heart is pleasing to God, then it will certainly be pleasing to man. Some people are beautiful on the outside, but their inside is rotten. Stand by thyself, come not near to me, for I am holier than thou. These are a smoke in my nose, the fire that burneth all the day (Isaiah 65:5). People are so religious that they even think that they are holier than others. They've been in church longer or known about God longer, but if they knew God and was trying to do his will, they wouldn't think that way. That's worldly thinking. Because people go to church every Sunday and run up and down the isles, don't mean they know God. We all know of certain people and have heard of certain people, but don't personally know them. And if you don't personally know them or know them in dept, we don't know them, we know of them. So because they've been in church longer does not mean God loves them any more than he loves you. If Christ return today and you have accepted him as your personal Savior just moments before, then you have the same right to the tree of life as someone who accepted him fifty years ago. Then Peter opened his mouth, and said, of a truth I perceive that God is no respector of persons: but in every nation he that feareth him, and worketh righteousness, is accepted with him. The word which God sent unto the children of Israel, preaching peace by Jesus Christ: (he is Lord of all) (Acts 10:34-36). God is letting us know he loves us all. Inspite of what we have or have not, he knows about your pass. We, no matter what one says, have done wrong in life. Some may have murdered a human, I'm specifying that because we all have killed something, maybe just an ant, but we killed and God said we shall not kill, and that mean nothing. Some have killed and because one have stole, he thinks his wrong is not as bad. In man's sight it's not, but to God sin is sin. There's no big sin or little sin. And the word says that the wages of sin is death; but the gift of God is eternal life through Jesus Christ our Lord (Romans 6:23). You see, God loves us inspite of our short comings. When we sin, we are forgiven the same way as the pastors, deacons, or anyone else, repentance. We are no less or no more than anyone else. Always know and believe that. You are just as important to God as anyone else. For God so loved the world, that he gave his only begotten son, that whosoever believeth in him should not perish, but have everlasting life (St. John 3:16). Nicodemus was a ruler of the Jews and he came to Jesus by night, and said unto him, rabbi, we know that thou art a teacher that come from God: for no man can do these miracles that one doest, except God be with him. Jesus answered and said unto him, verily, verily, I say unto thee, except a man be born again, he cannot see the kingdom of God (St. John 3:1-3). Nicodemus was a ruler, a man of the Pharisees, set in high places, but he must go through Jesus as you and I to get to Heaven and I'm glad it's like that. He's no less or more than we are. Jesus had a friend named Lazarus of Bethany, the brother of Mary, who anointed the Lord with ointment, and wiped his feet with her hair. Lazarus was sick and his sister sent for Jesus, saying Lord, behold, he whom thou lovest is sick. When Jesus heard about Lazarus he stayed where he was for two more days. They thought that because Jesus loved him and was his friend, he would run to him, but Jesus didn't and Lazarus died. You see some people think because they have been in church longer than you or give more money, God will answer their prayers before he answer yours. But what one must understand is what Jesus will do for others he will do for you. It's because he loves all of us and he's all of our friend. We are no less or no more than anyone. And this was an example for us. Sometimes we're disobedient and sometimes we make promises we don't keep. I recall when Peter said Lord, I am ready to go with thee, both into prison and to death. And the Lord said I tell thee, Peter, the cock shalt not crow this day, before that thou shalt thrice deny that thou knowest me (St. Luke 22:33-34). And as always, just as the Lord said, it came to pass. But what I love about Jesus is, we sometimes do him wrong, but he want do us wrong. This is where love comes to play. We know that Peter was one of the twelve disciples, as a matter of fact, he was looked at as the leader. When Jesus had risen, the angel told them to go your way, tell his disciples and Peter that he goeth before you into Galilee: there shall ye see him, as he said unto you (St. Mark 16:6-7). They knew Peter was a disciple, but because he denied the Lord as the Lord said, he had to separate Peter from the disciples to let Peter know that he loves him just as much as the other disciples. He was letting Peter know that he was no less or no more than the other disciples. Now I tell you do not measure your worth by others possessions or position, but by what thous saith the Lord. In the sight of the Lord, the poor is no less than the rich, the old is no less than the young, and the female is no less than male. Always remember; I'm no less or no more than anyone else.

Thank you Lord! Thank you for loving us all the same.

Thanks be unto God our creator, Jesus Christ our Savior,
And the Holy Spirit our Comforter.

AMEN!

Chapter 10
I'm a true child of God

Again, when you know whose you are, then you will know who you are. So I, without a doubt know that I'm a true child of God. If one know nothing about life, he needs to know who he serve. And I'm not talking about tomorrow, because as we know, it is not promised on this side. But there is a tomorrow even if it's on the other side. The word says: now therefore fear the Lord, and serve him in sincerity and in truth: and put away the Gods which your father served on the other side of the flood, and in Eygpt; and serve ye the Lord. And if it seem evil unto you to serve the Lord, then choose you this day whom ye will serve; whether the Gods which your fathers served that were on the other side of the flood, or the Gods of the Amorites, in whose land ye dwell: but as for me and my house, we will serve the Lord (Joshua 24:14-15). We must understand, God doesn't give us choices, he gives us commandments, we make choices. My choice is, and I hope others is also, I'm going to serve the only true and living God. The God of Abraham, Isaac, and Jacob. When one get sick or in trouble or just need some comfort, they can call on the name of Jesus, the most powerful name on Earth and Heaven, and get some results. But if you call on other Gods, you will just keep on waiting for an answer or some healing, or just see if they will talk back to you. I serve a God who is able to supply my every need according to his riches in glory, by Christ Jesus (Philippians 4:19). If people who is serving other Gods just look at the situation around them, they would understand if their God is in a building, how then if they travel to another state or even another town or even one street over can their God be with them if he's still in the building? The God I serve is omnipresence (universal presence, everywhere at all times). If I travel out of state or out of country, my God is with me. No matter where I go, I will serve him. I don't have to look at my picture that is in my cell phone to know my God is present. All I have to do is call on his name. He's present and listening. How do I know? I can't speak for anyone else but for me, his words abides in me. If ye abide in me, and my words abide in you, ye shall ask what ye will, and it shall be done unto you (St. John 15:7). If a man love me, he will keep my words: and my father will love him and we will come onto him, and make our abode with him (St. John 14:23). In the beginning was the word, and the word was with God, and the word was God (St. John 1:1). I'm trusting in the word which means I'm trusting in God. Because I've accepted Christ as my personal Savior and his words abide in me. I know without a doubt, he's forever present with me. I know I'm a true child of God! You'll know that you're a true child of God when you confess with your mouth and truly believe in your heart the Lord Jesus and that God raised him from the dead. I heard a pastor ask his congregation to repeat after him: that Christ died and was raised from the dead, then he told them that everyone that confessed that was saved, and I knew that was not true. But we are human, we make mistakes, but he spoke it again. I knew that if there was someone witnessing, they was wrong too. What made that wrong is because confessing is not enough. You have to truly believe it in your heart. For with the heart man believeth unto righteousness; and with the mouth confession is made unto salvation (Romans 10:10). We must preach and teach the word the way that God intended, not the way we want to put it. Whatever I do for God, I want God to lead because it will be right. We as professed children of God know that sometimes pastors, deacons, and mothers are speaking from their knowledge. Some have gone to Theology School and if one choose to do so, that's fine. But as for me, I'm going to study my Bible (King James Version) and if there's something I don't know, I'll call on the Lord. For the Lord giveth wisdom: out of his mouth comes knowledge and understanding (Proverbs 2:6). I've learned that God will give you wisdom thru a child or sometimes thru other's sermons. Going to school is fine, one may tell you, not that it's right, what day Jesus brothers and sisters were born. They can pinpoint the exact location where he was born. Now they're saying he had a son and was married. Yet they can't find a cure for a common cold. They pay for this education, when God's word is free. It makes them look and sound well educated, but when you speak or if you do a sermon and the least that can understand don't, your message is almost in vain to some and totally in vain to others. I don't stand before God's people to entertain, but to encourage. We don't need foolishness, we need faith and how do we get faith? By truly preaching, teaching, and studying God's word. So then faith cometh by hearing, and hearing by the word of God (Romans 10:17). It's irrelevant how many rocks Jesus threw when he was a child. We know he played in the sand because when they brought the woman to be stoned, he was drawing in the sand. But what is relevant is when he began teaching in the Synagogue and alone the highways. His preaching and teaching was letting people know what was necessary for them to do if they wanted to live right and live eternal. Jesus and the prophets used simple, easy to understand words and sometimes parables. A parable is like a story to give one a picture so that they can understand better. Jesus preached and taught to everyone. We wonder why people leave the church that they have been attending for years. Some leave because of the relocation of their Job or their family, but those who leave and you have no idea why, start looking at the officers of the church, look at the activities of the church, look at your collection activity, look at the favortism in your church, and if you can't find it there, then ask God to reveal it to you. I remember blind Bartimaeus setting beside the highway begging and began to cry out for mercy (St. Mark 10: 46-52). He was content with begging, but when he heard about Jesus coming alone, he forgot about his contentment with begging and began to cry out for mercy. And just as people tried to get him to stop crying out for Jesus, they are still doing it today. If you don't have money or some high standard, pastors some not all of us don't recognize you. I truly, and anyone that worship with us will tell you, I don't care if your rich or poor, black or white, male or female, tall or short, believer or non believer, I treat everyone the same. I know I'm a true child of God. When people cry out to God we must help them. People are doing any and everything because they don't know Jesus and because of their lifestyle, we want to turn them back. Jesus said, they that are whole need not a physician; but they that are sick. I came not to call the righteous, but sinners to repentance (St. Luke 5:31-32). So when we whom God call to preach and teach his word stop worrying about who has the most members, who has the biggest church, and who drives what and how much money one has and start lifting up the name of Jesus the way he ask, so he can do the drawing so lives can be changed and saved then the world would be a better place to live. Trust in God, live so he can use you, and let your light so shine before men, that they may see your good works, and glorify your father which is in Heaven (St. Matthew 5:16).

Thanks be unto God for his inspirations.
I know I'm a true child of God.

Thanks be unto God our Father, Jesus Christ our Savior, and the Holy Spirit our Comforter.

AMEN

Printed in the United States
126351LV00003B/1/P